Eat The Bunny
Before the Bunny Eats You

WORDS & DESIGN BY: SCOTT BACHMANN

ILLUSTRATED BY: SARAH WILKINSON

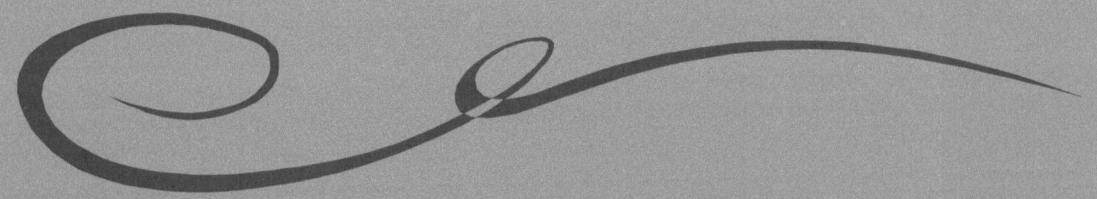

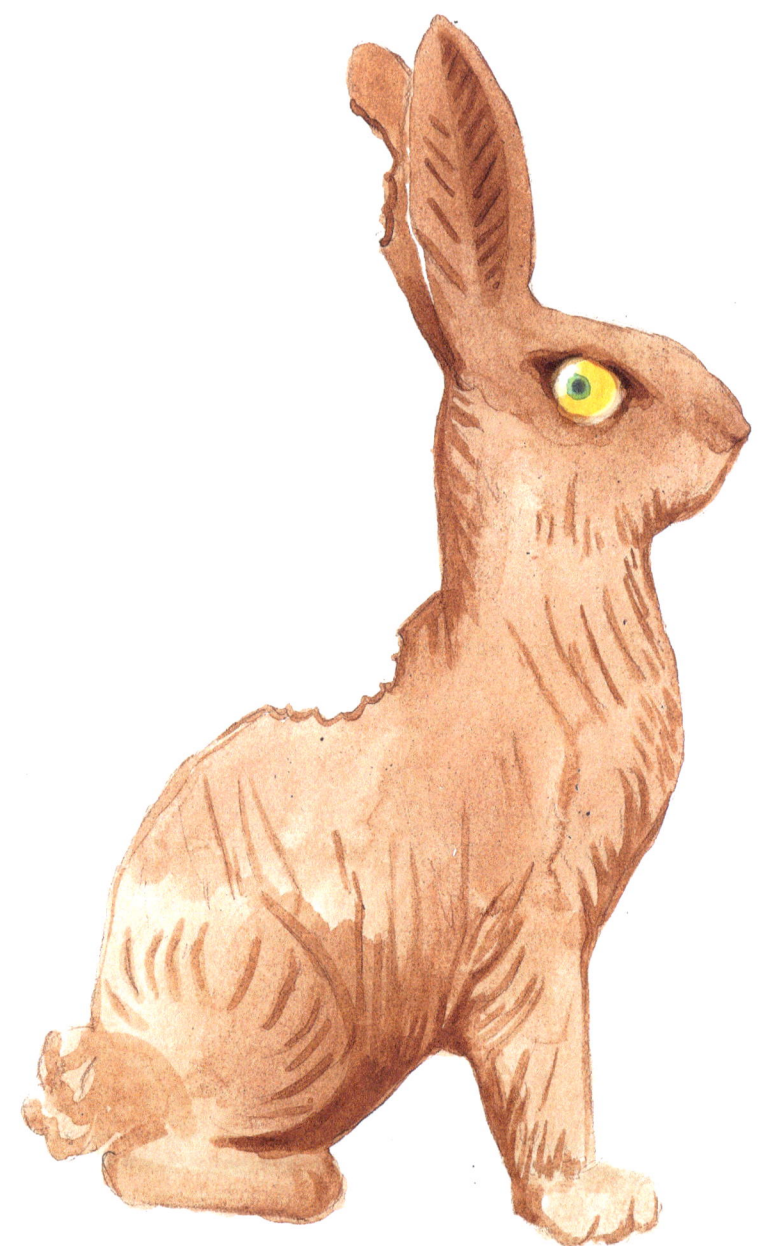

ISBN: 1478203838
ISBN-13: 978-1478203834

DEDICATION

Nigel -who brought Sarah around
Anita, Diana, Janine - who helped hone the idea
Candy eyed chocolate easter bunnies for looking creepy but tasting delicious

ACKNOWLEDGMENTS

Cover photo of Sarah Wilkinson by
Albertine Feurer-Young Photography
ArtOfAlbertine.com

Interior portrait of Sarah Wilkinson by
Sarah Wilkinson

Cover photo of Scott Bachmann by
Anita Bachmann

Interior photo of Scott Bachmann by
Ashley Delilah Lane

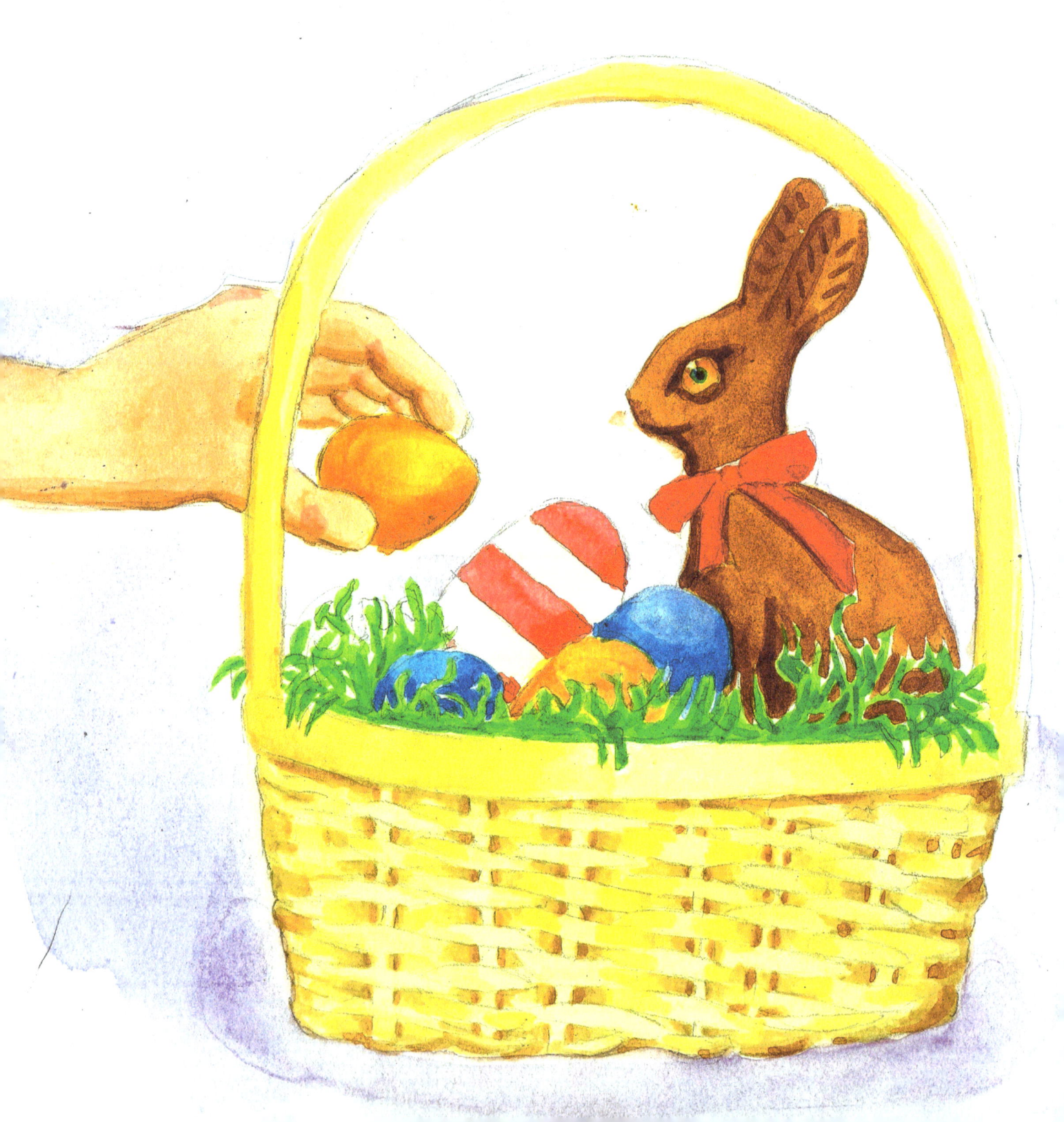

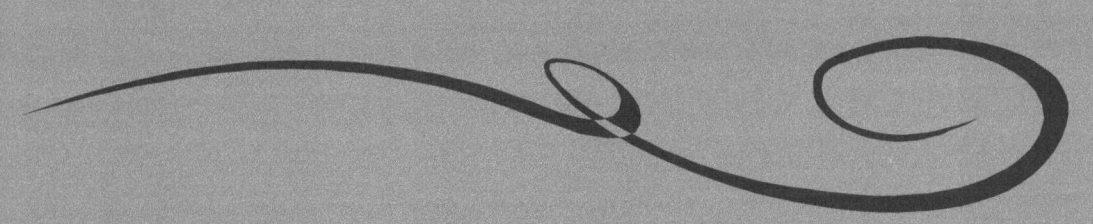

WE MADE COLORED EGGS
AND BUNNIES OF BROWN
BUT SOMETHING WAS WRONG
WHEN EASTER CAME ROUND

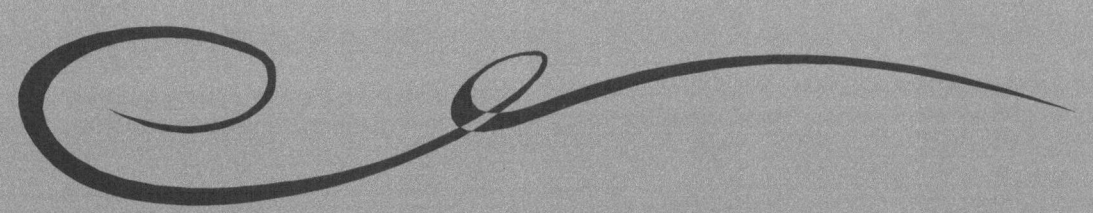

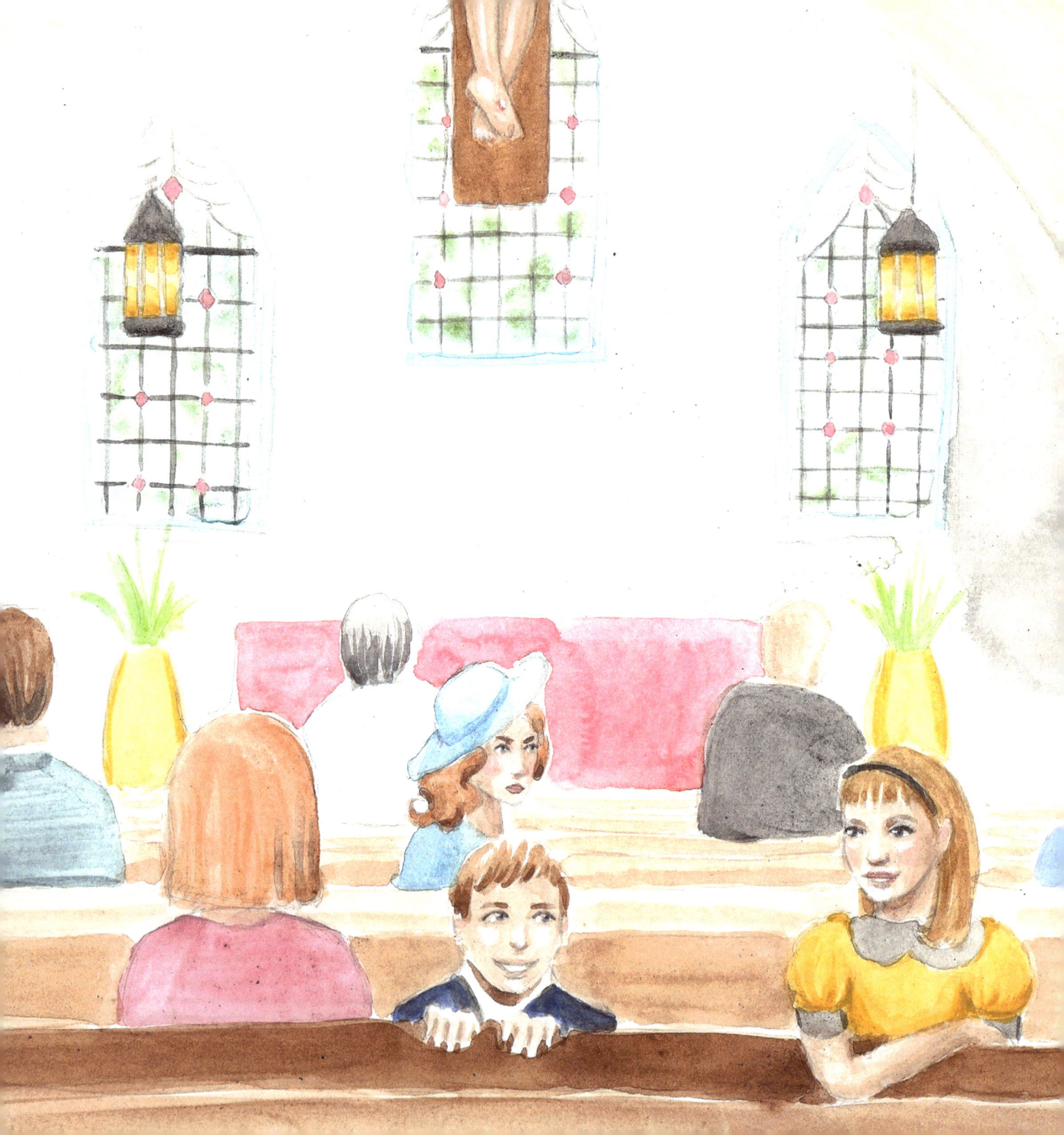

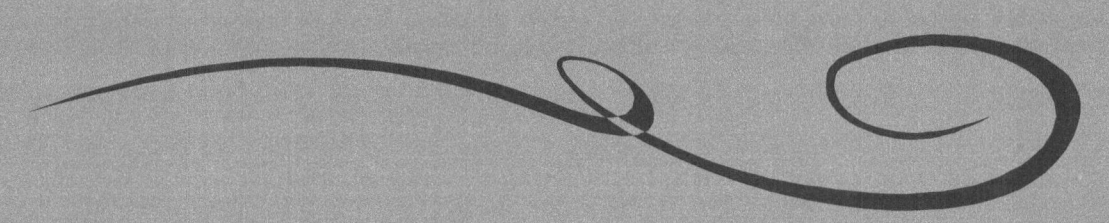

We donned our bright bonnets
We wore fancy dress
For a holiday about murder
Betrayal and duress

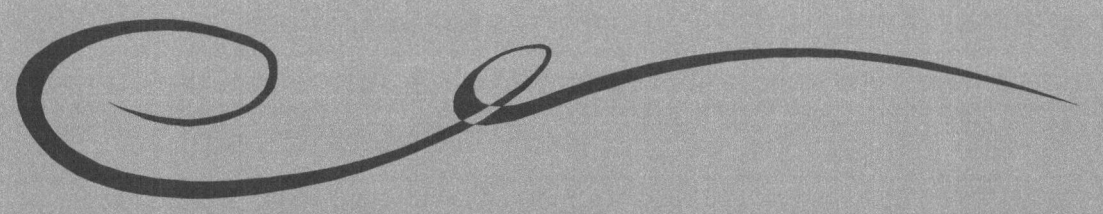

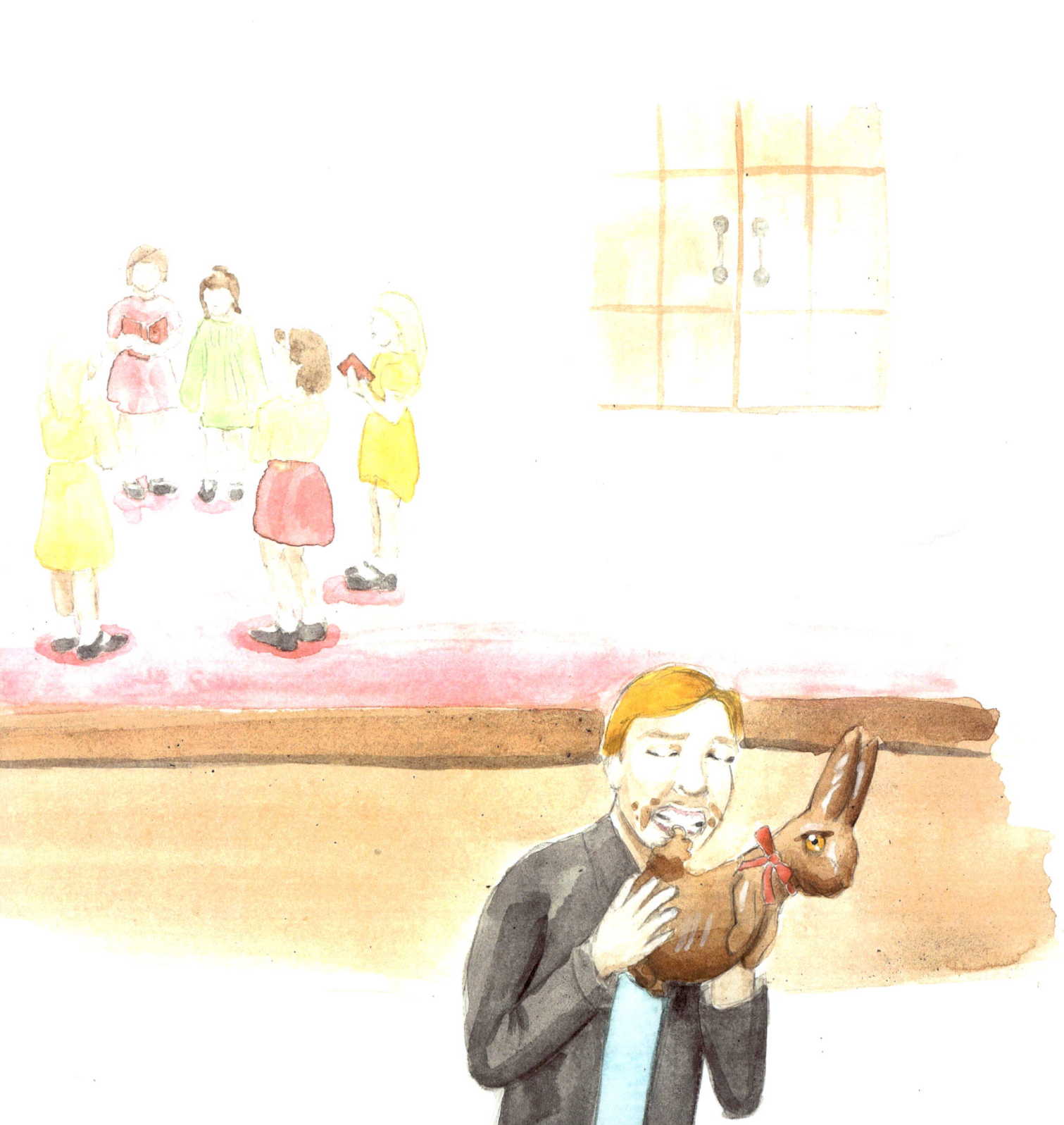

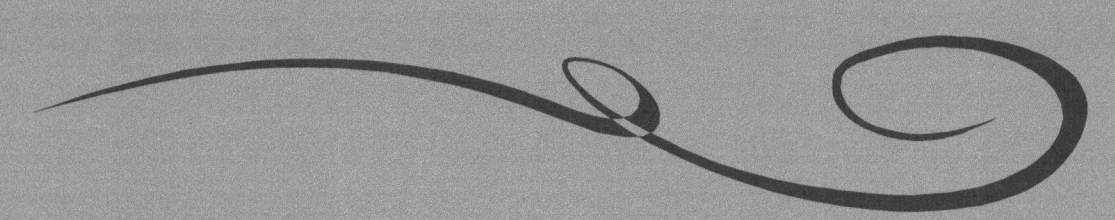

FOR THE ONE WHO'S ARISEN

WE SING OUT IN GLEE

AND CELEBRATE BY EATING

OUR CHOCOLATE BUNNIES

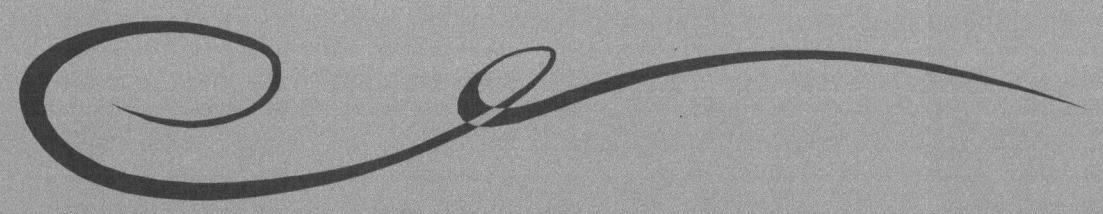

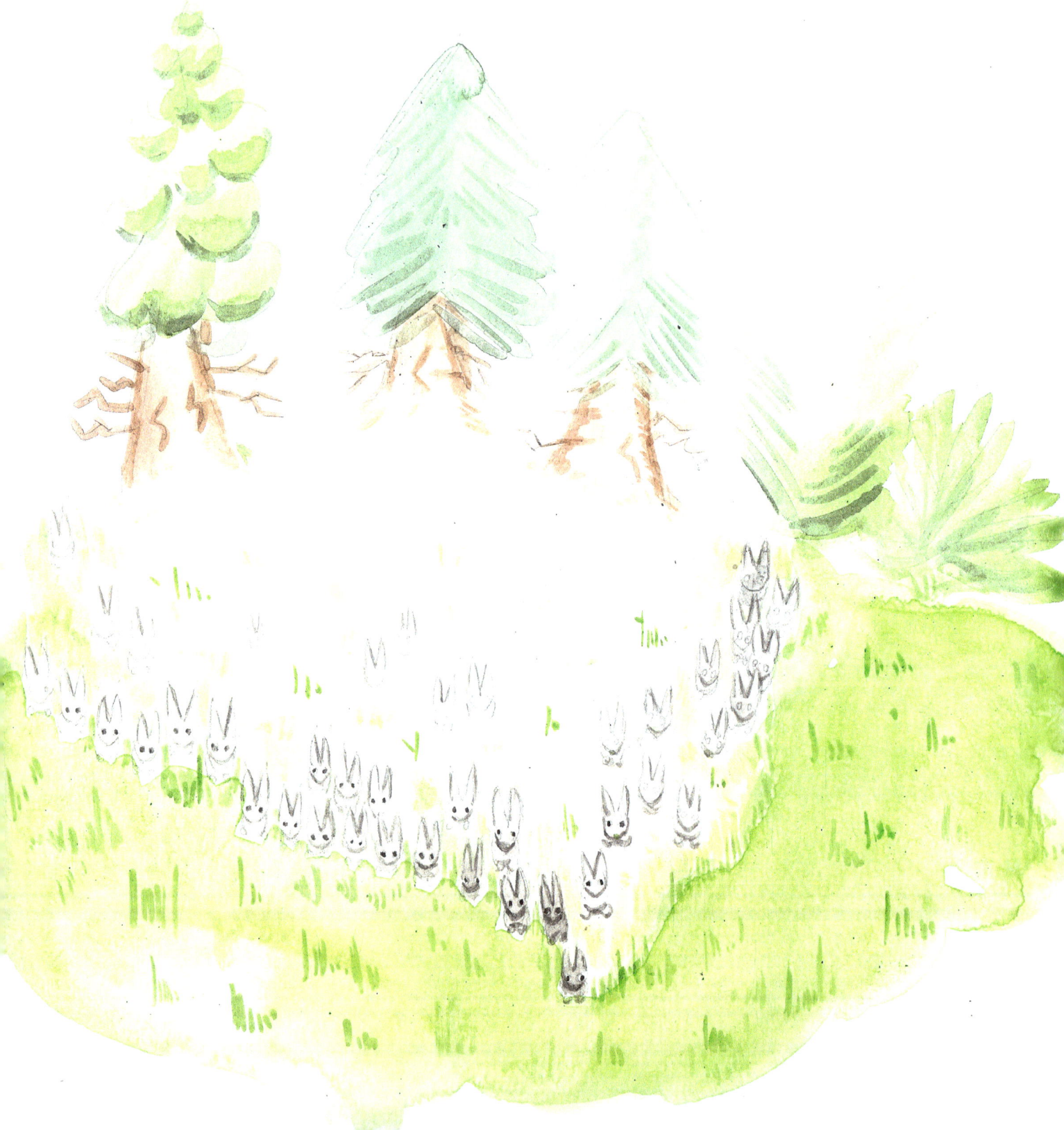

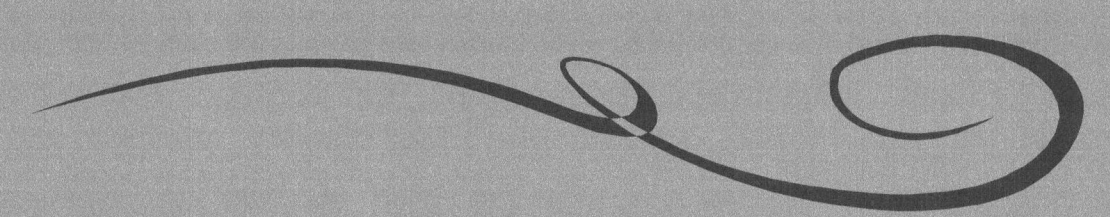

BUT THAT BUNNY'S A SYMBOL

OF PAGAN REBIRTH

OF LIFE'S MAD DESIRE TO

BLANKET THE EARTH

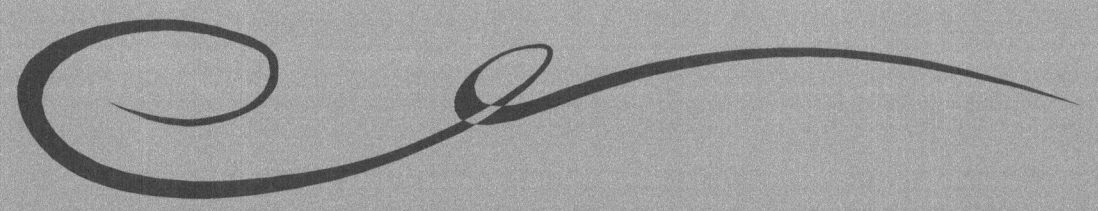

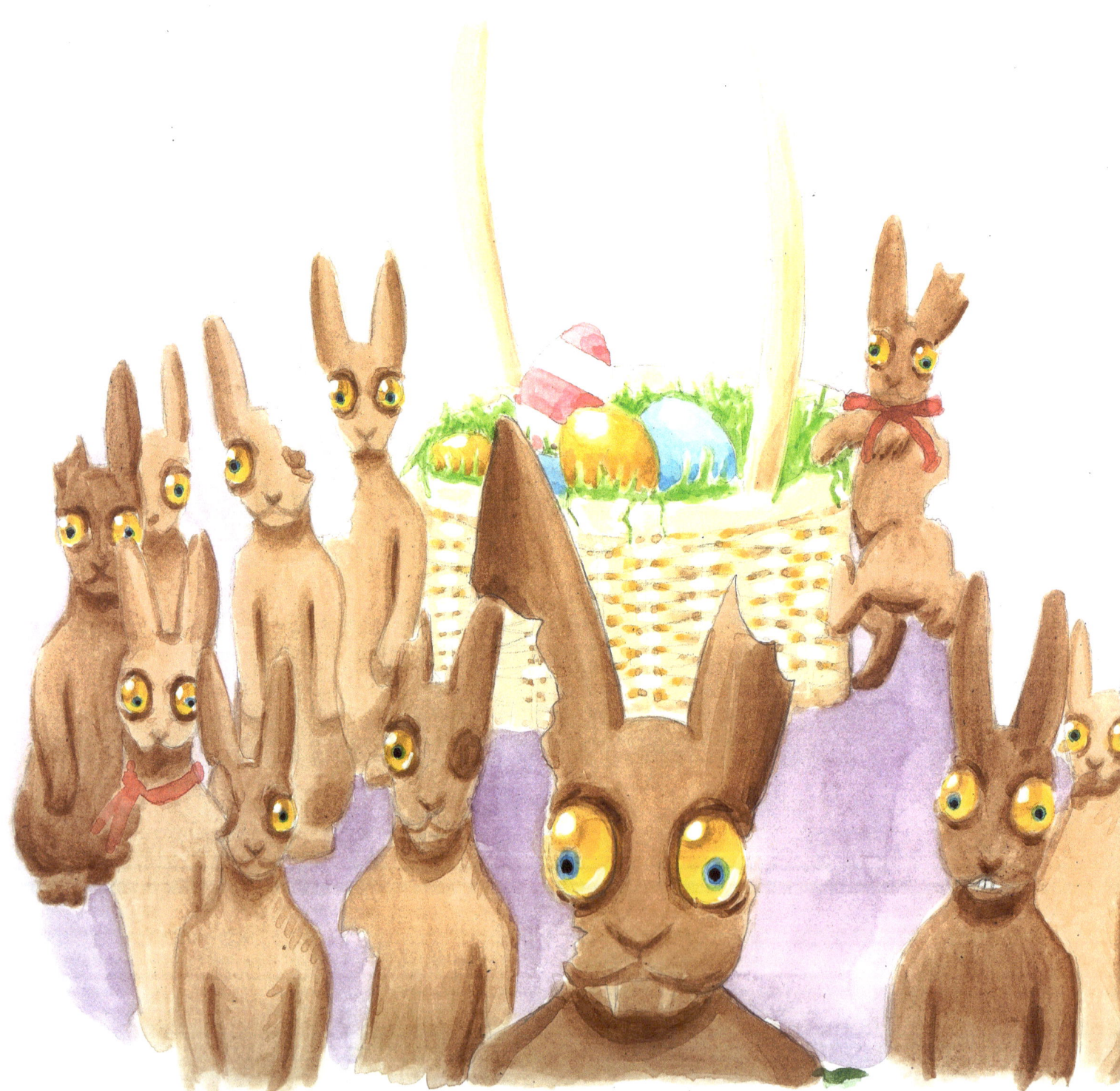

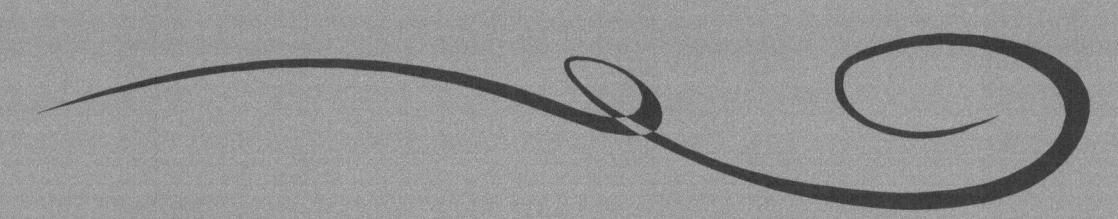

WHEN THE MIRACLE HAPPENED

WE SHOULD HAVE FORESEEN

THE BUNNIES AWAKENED

HUNGRY AND MEAN

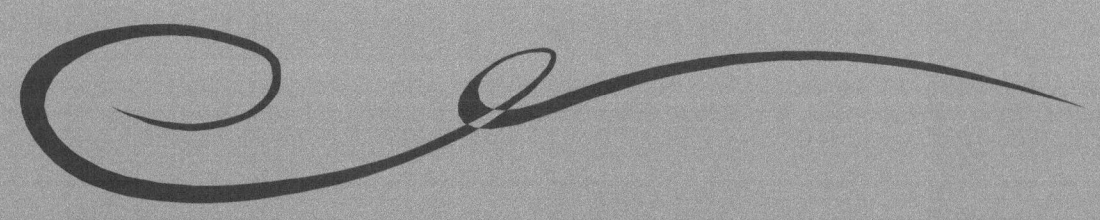

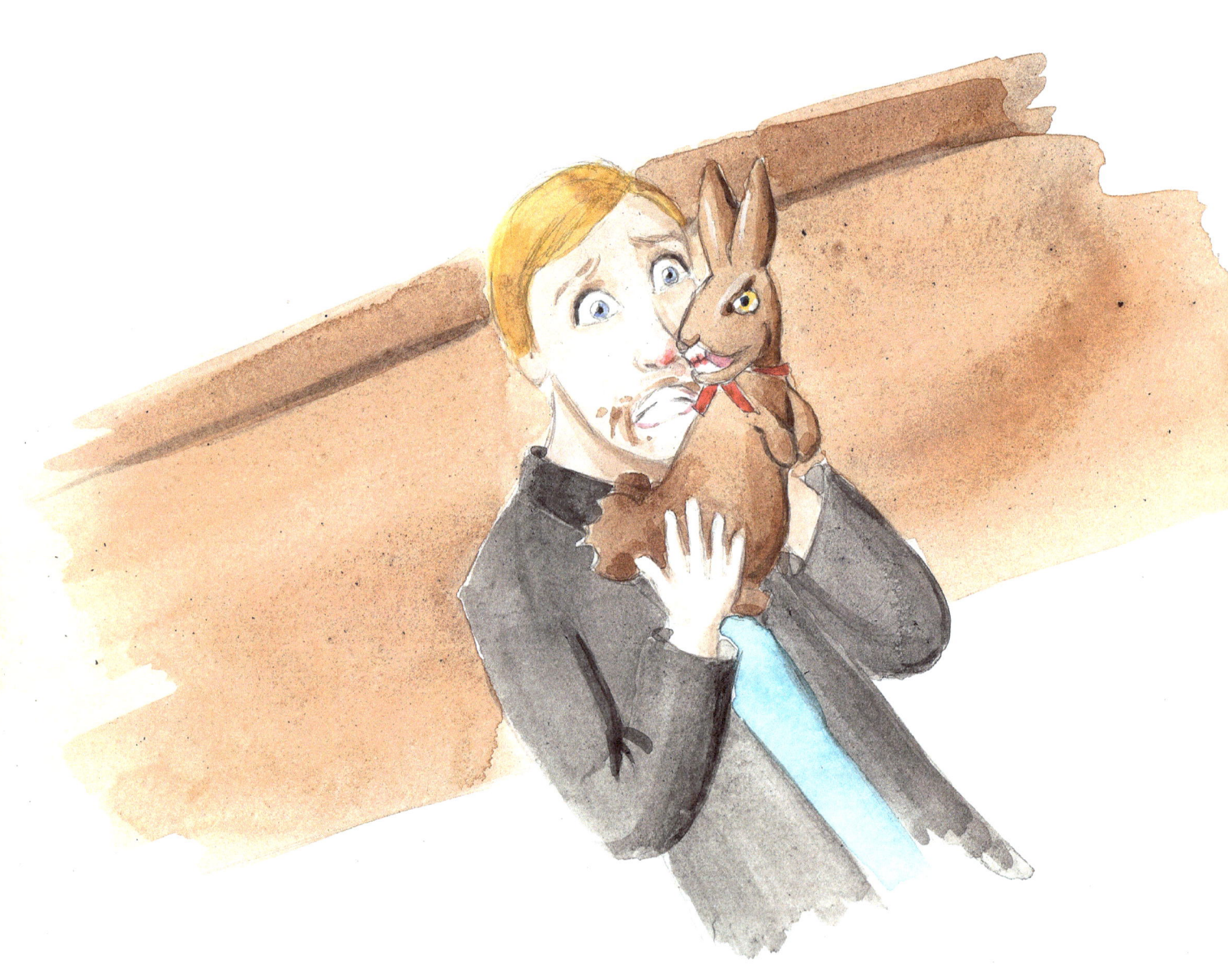

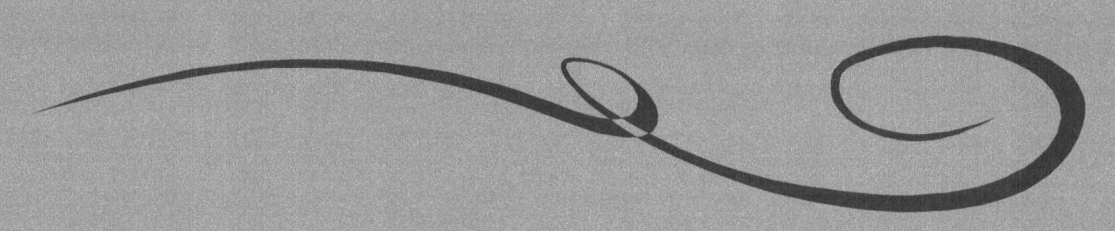

WE BIT OFF THEIR BOTTOMS

THEY DID NOT APPROVE

NOW THEY HUNGER FOR US

WE'D ALL BETTER MOVE

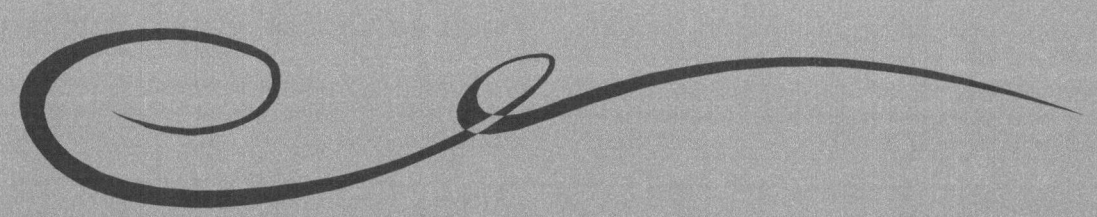

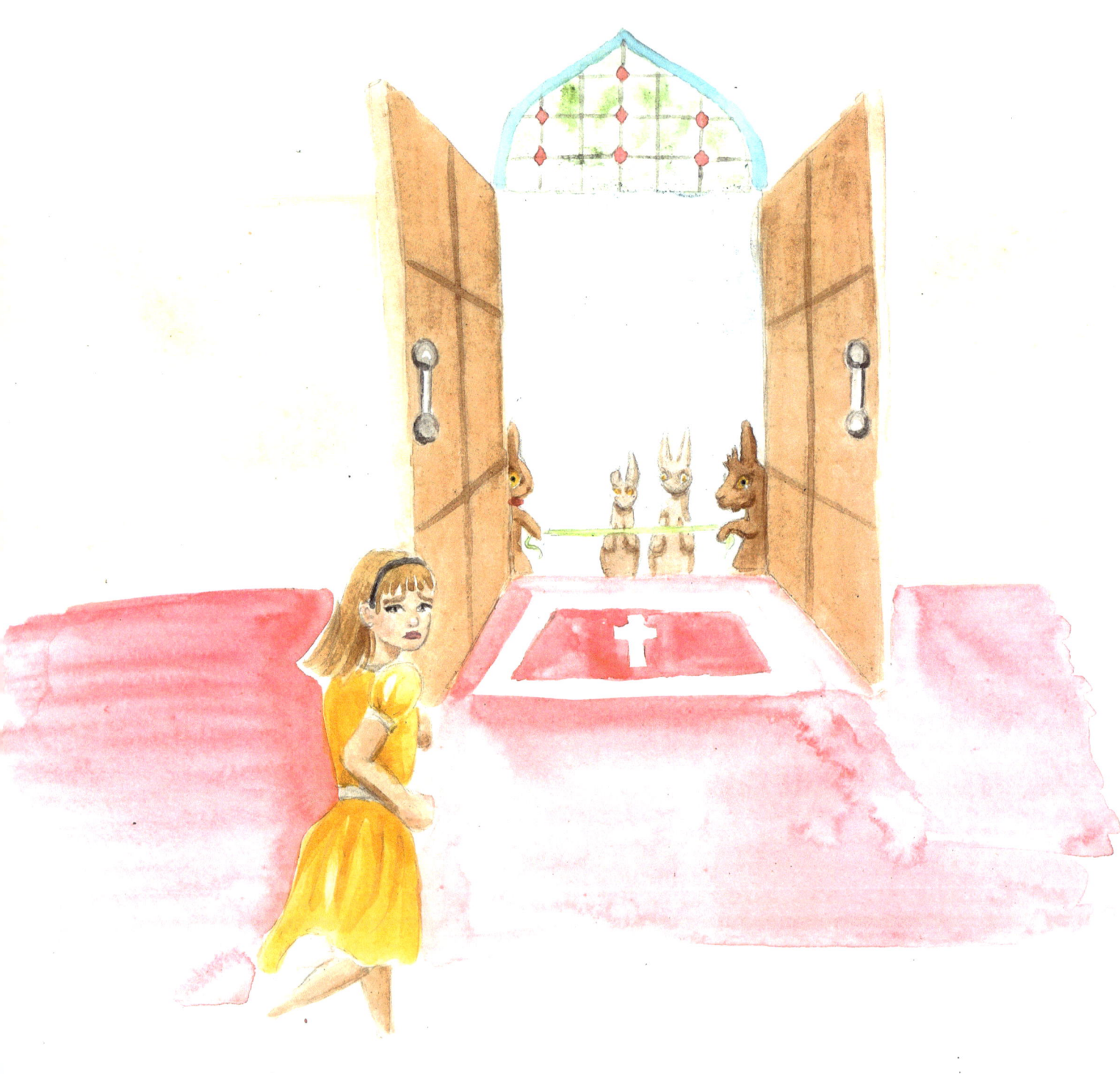

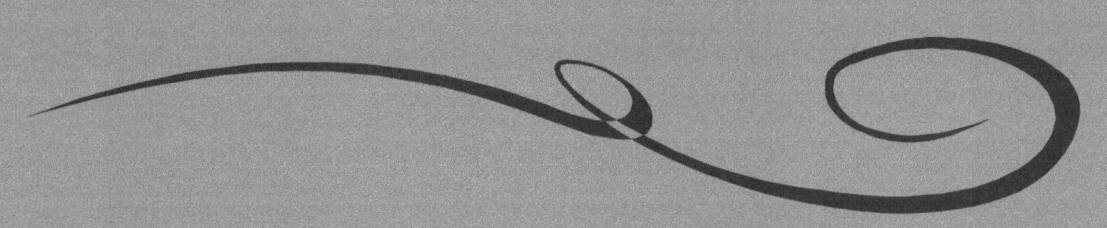

OH RUN OH RUN
AS FAST AS YOU CAN,
BUNNIES ARE QUICK
AND THEY KNOW HOW TO PLAN

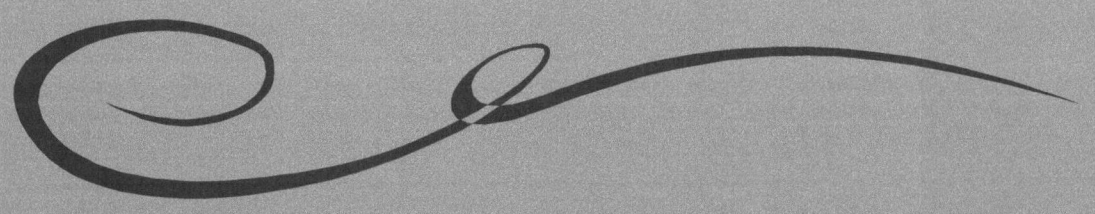

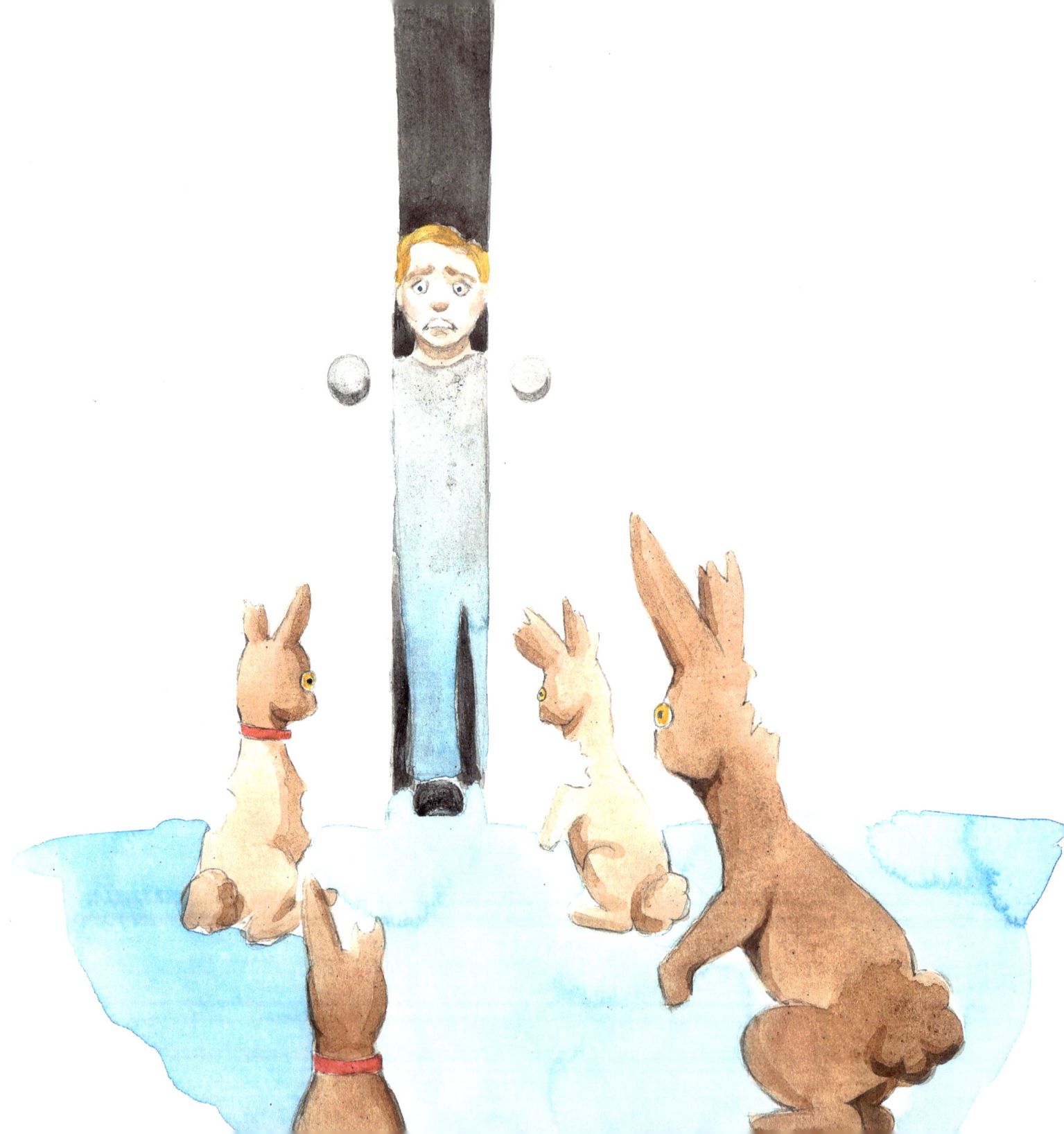

TRAPPED IN A CORNER
WHAT CAN YOU DO
EXCEPT TO EAT THEM
BEFORE THEY EAT YOU

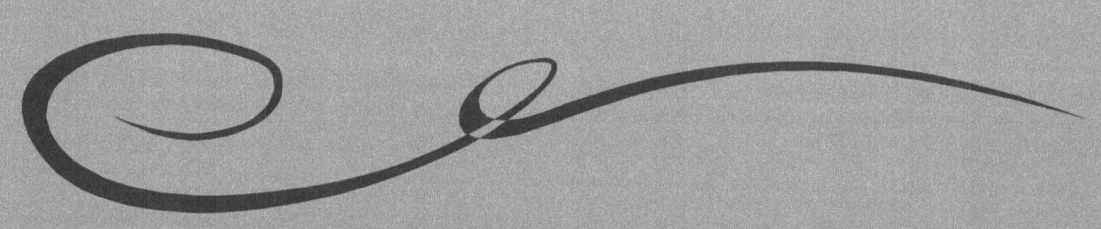

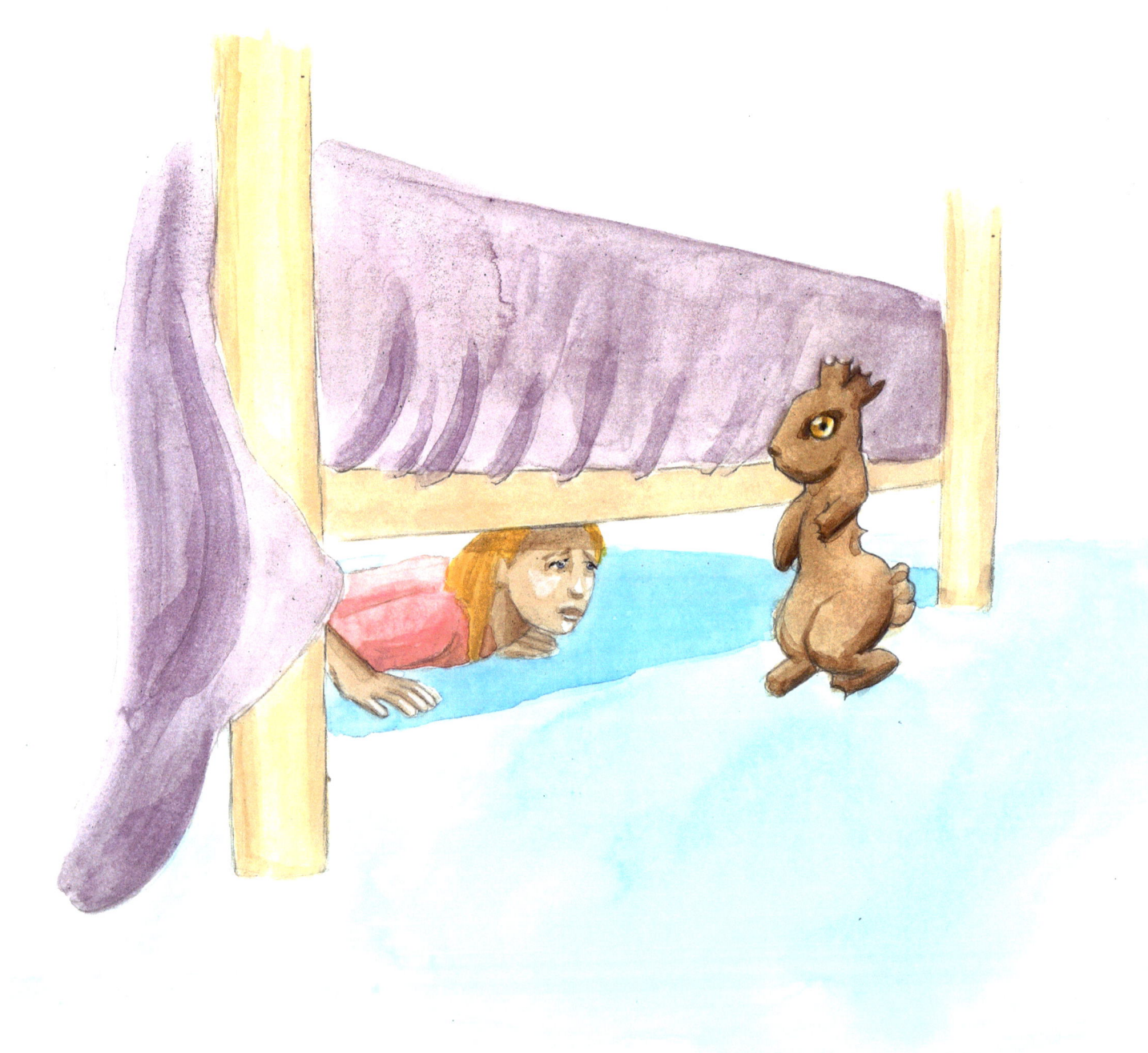

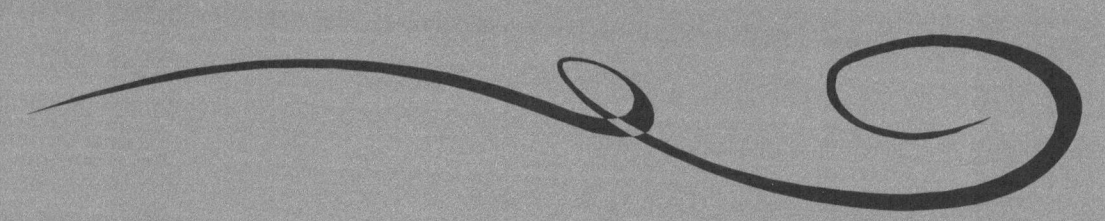

Don't bother with tails
I have to be blunt
Without ears they can't hear
Without feet they can't hunt

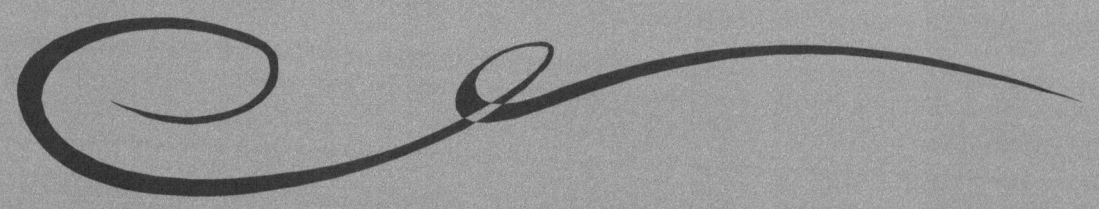

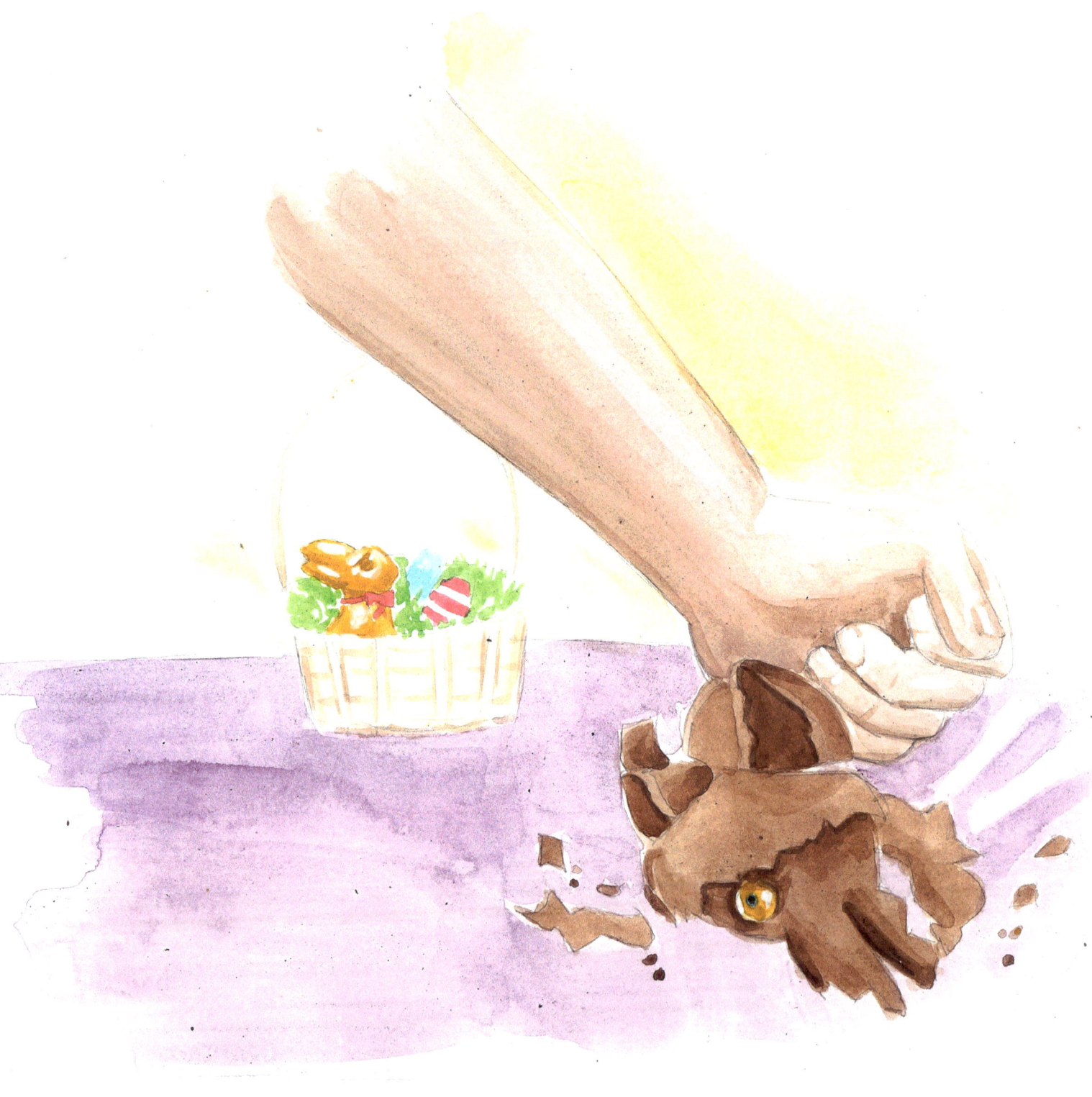

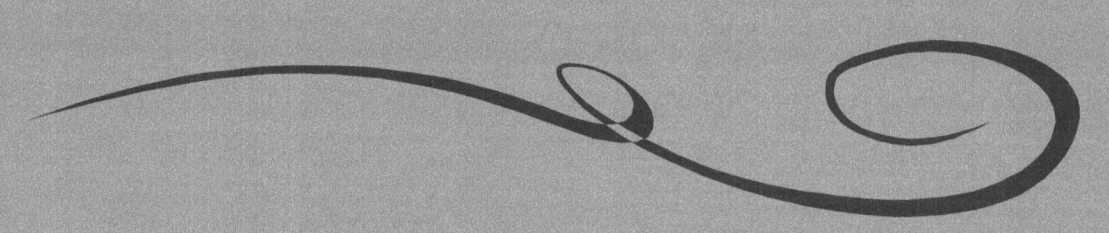

BIND THEM IN FOIL

THEN THEY CAN'T MOVE

BREAK THEM IF HOLLOW

YOU STRIKE ON THE GROOVE

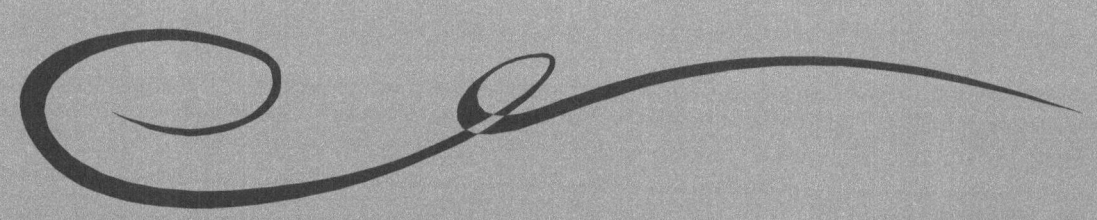

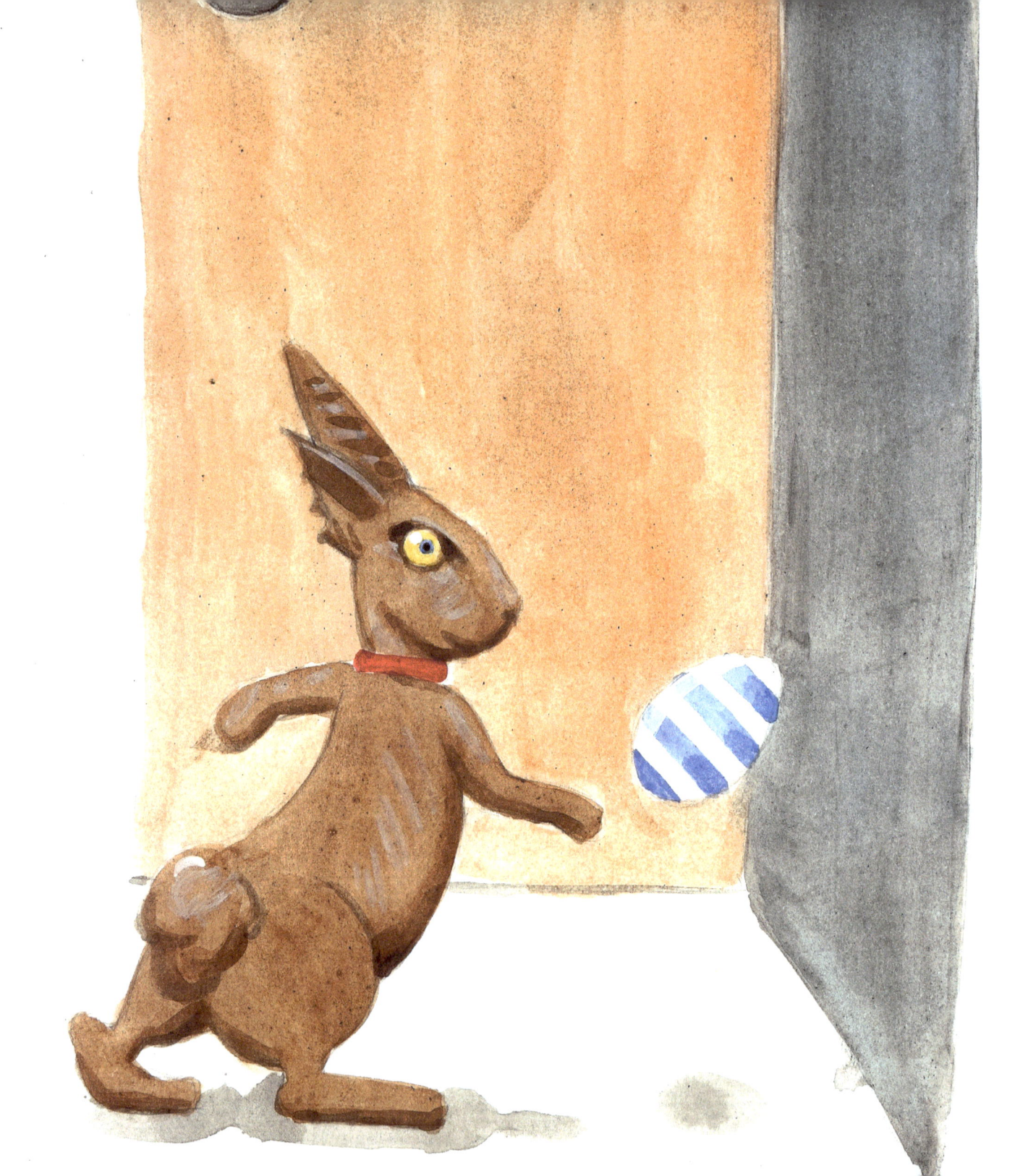

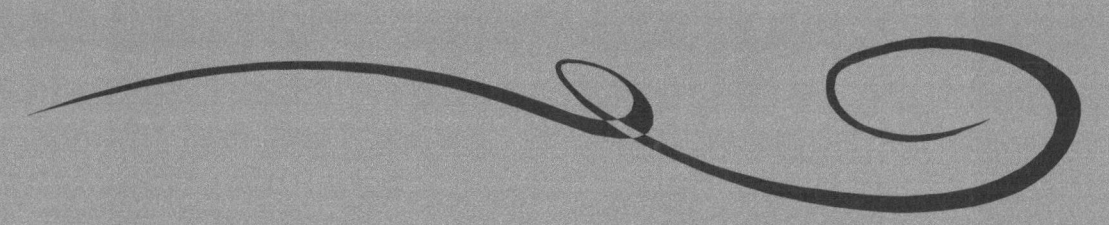

Look for the eggs
They leave on their trail
Then hop for your life
You run without fail

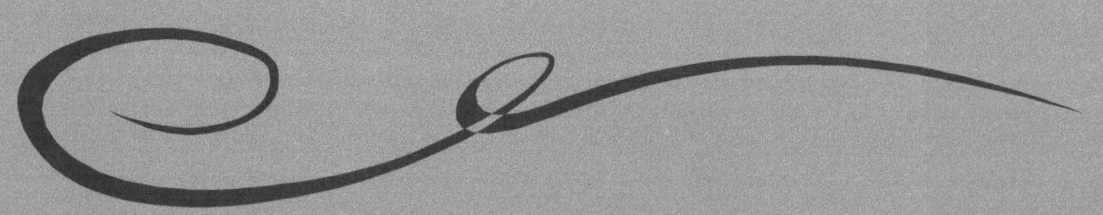

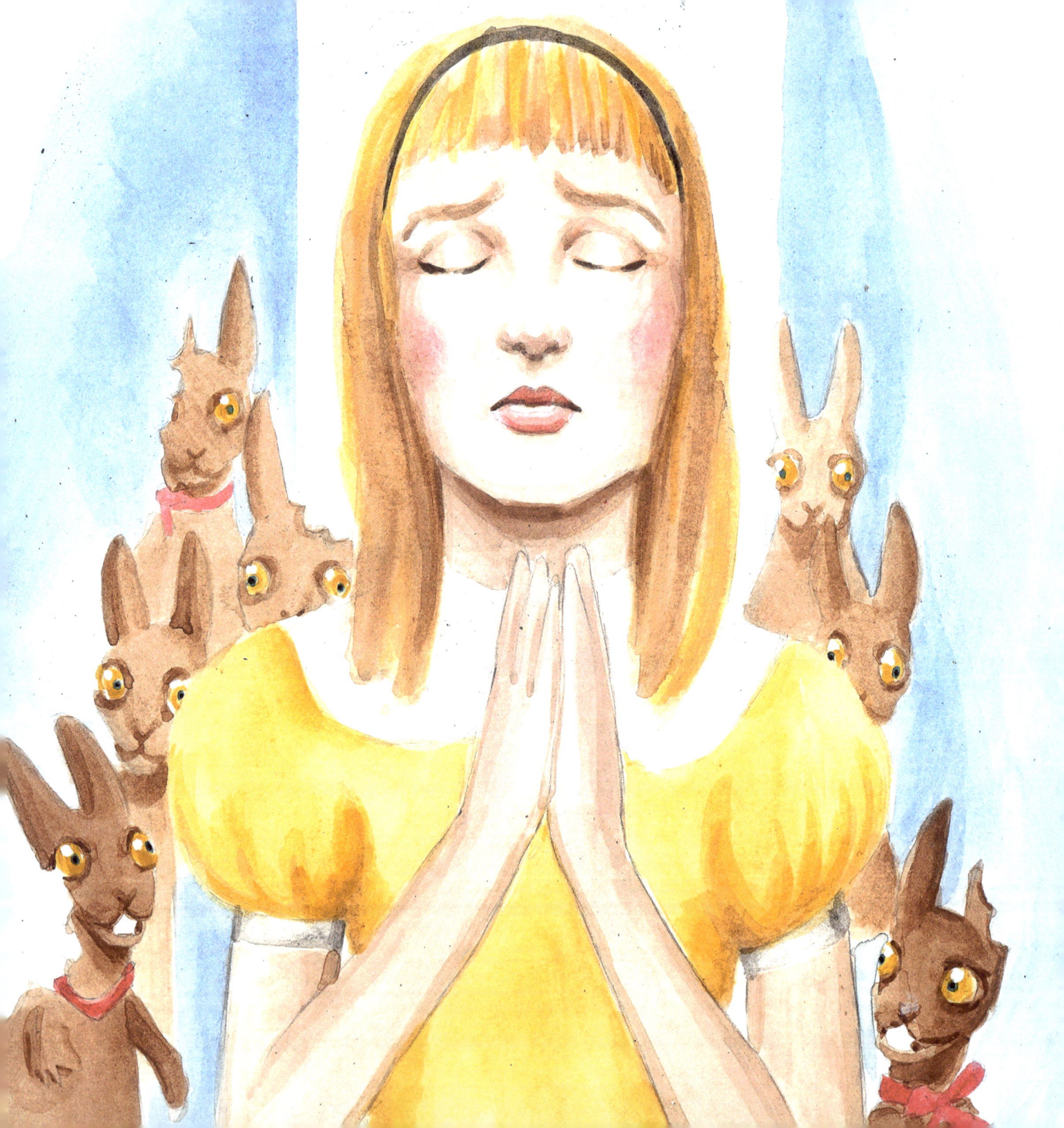

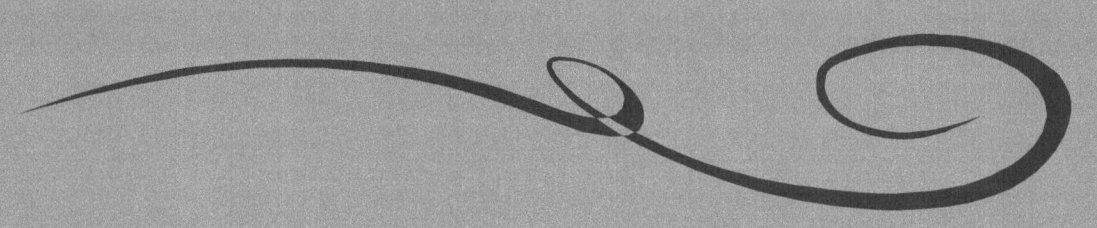

You hide until Lent

Is used up and spent

Confess all your sins

Repent and repent

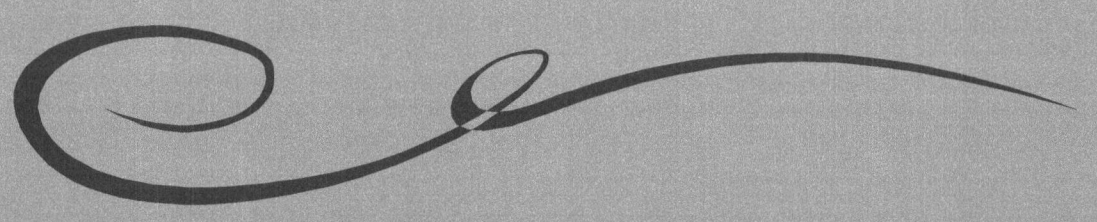

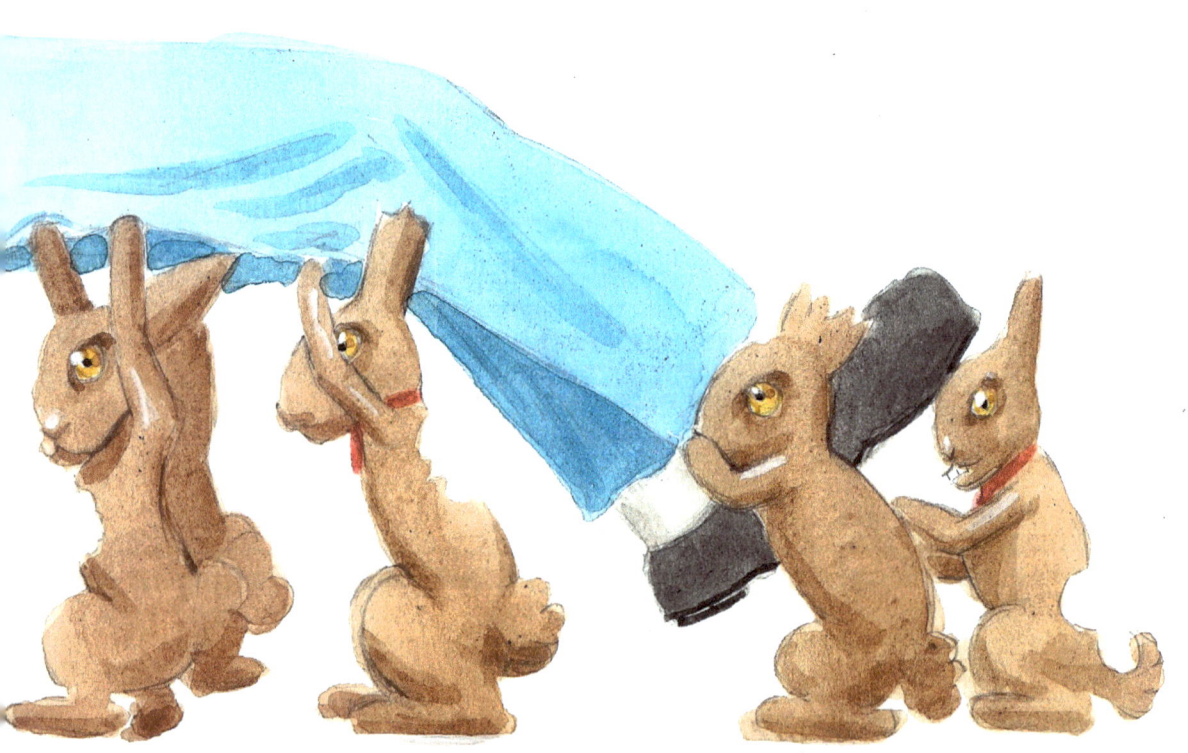

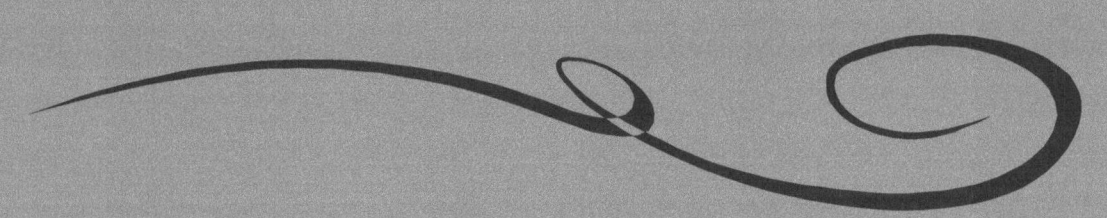

And maybe, just maybe
You will be spared
And not the one tripped
To be left behind scared

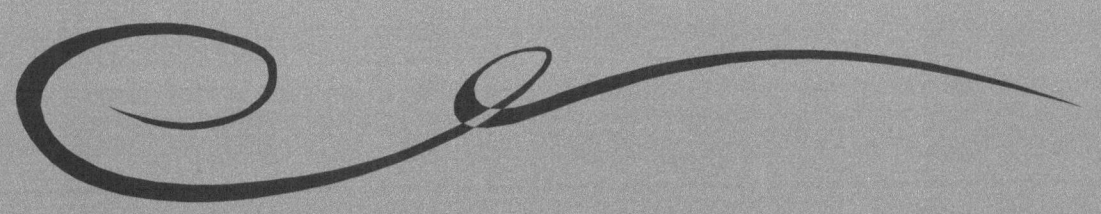

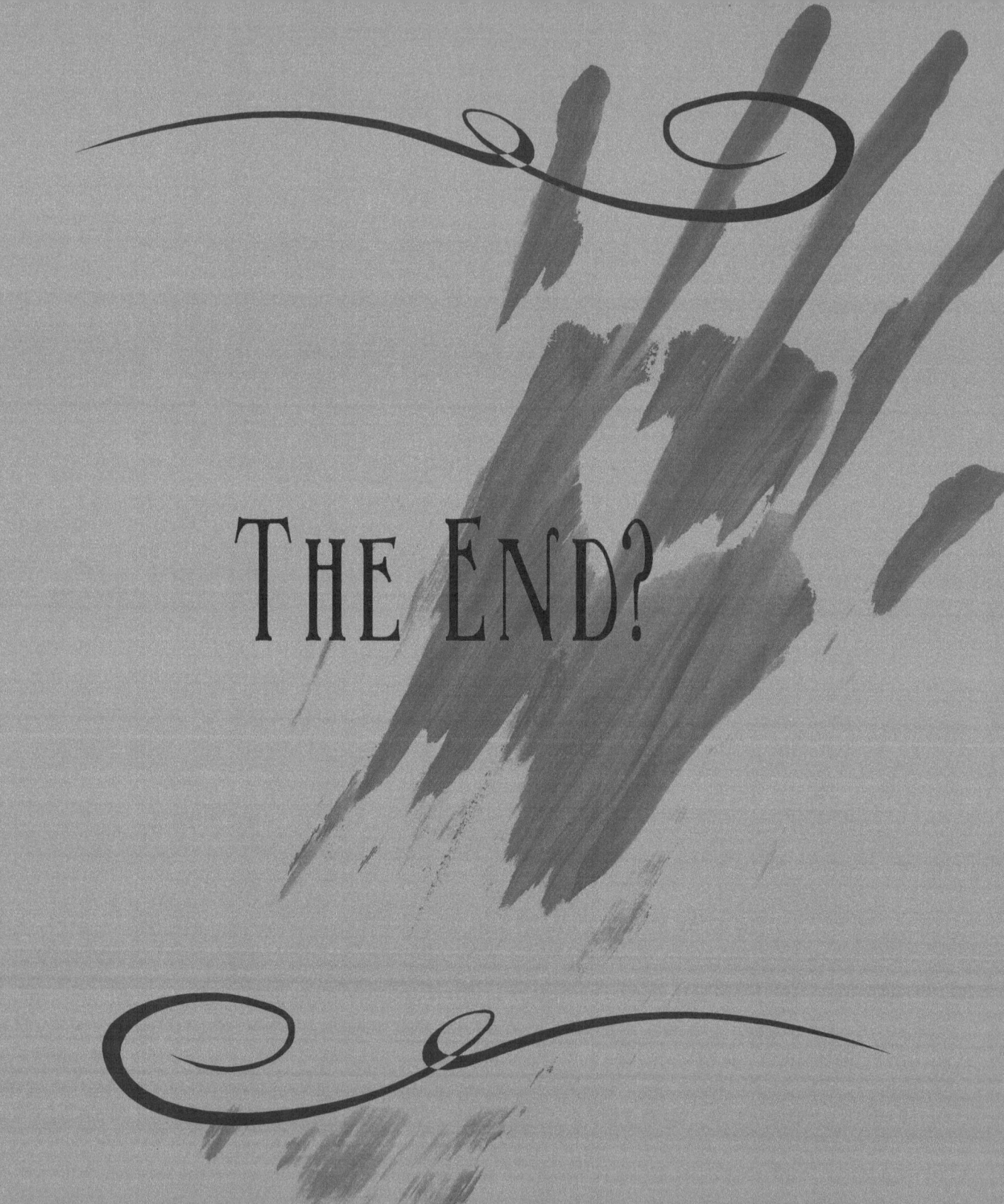

THE END?

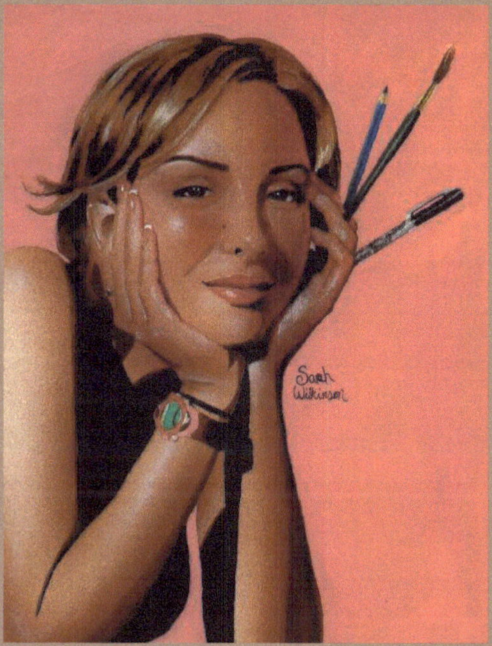

ABOUT THE ILLUSTRATOR

Sarah Wilkinson
I am a full time illustrator and sketch card artist! I love what I do. In my 7 year professional career, I have worked with MANY properties including: Star Wars, Lord Of The Rings, Star Trek, My Little Pony, Indiana Jones, Iron Man movies 1 and 2 (lots of card work with Marvel), and many more!

http://sarahwilkinson.deviantart.com/
http://www.facebook.com/SarahWilkinsonArt
http://www.sarahwilkinson.net/

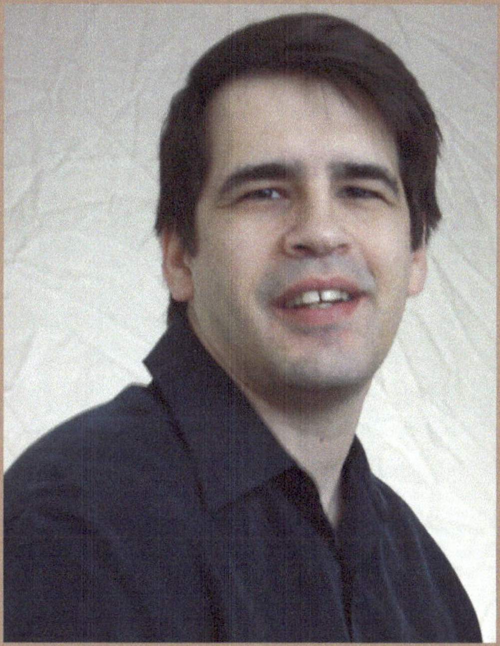

ABOUT THE WRITER

Scott Bachmann writes novels and comics when his cat isn't in the way of his keyboard. Scott has two grown boys and a very tolerant wife.
http://scottcomics.com

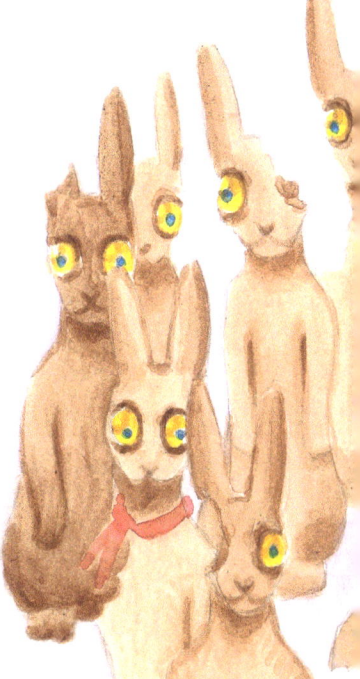

www.ingramcontent.com/pod-product-compliance
Lightning Source LLC
Chambersburg PA
CBHW041304180526
45172CB00003B/958